저 높은
곳을 향하여

Towards that high place

저 높은 곳을 향하여
Towards that high place

발 행 | 2024년 04월 12일
저 자 | 이상근
펴낸이 | 한건희
펴낸곳 | 주식회사 부크크
출판사등록 | 2014.07.15.(제2014-16호)
주 소 | 서울특별시 금천구 가산디지털1로 119 SK트윈타워 A동 305
호
전 화 | 1670-8316
이메일 | info@bookk.co.kr

ISBN | 979-11-410-8060-0

www.bookk.co.kr

이상근 한·영 대역시집
Poems of Sang-geun Lee A New Collection

저 높은 곳을 향하여
Towards that high

place

이상근 지음
Written by Lee Sang-geun

작가의 말

누구나 앞만 보고 열심히 살아온 인생이라고 말한다. 이 세상에 태어나서 언제 생을 마감할는지는 모르겠지만, 앞일을 설계하고 그에 상당한 노력을 하고 산다.

이름 3자 명예를 남기려고 애쓰는 사람이 있고 재물을 일구어서 자식에게 기대를 걸고 유산을 남기려고 애쓰는 사람이 있는가 하면 오직 자기만의 즐거운 취미생활과 건강을 위하는 사람도 있다.

여러 부류의 삶 중에 나는 어느 부류에 속하는지 나 자신도 잘 모르지만 열심히 살아왔다. 인생 70여 고개를 훌쩍 넘기면서 나에게도 시詩라는 것이 몇 편 쓰였다. 남들이 보았을 때는 별것 아니게 보일는지 몰라도 나는 최선을 다하여 글을 써보았다.

나는 아날로그 시대 교육을 받고 70여 년을 살아온 사람인데 시詩가 60여 편이 되어갈 때쯤 사진과 영상이 나의 눈에 보인다. 시를 쓰면서 찍은 사진을 보기도 하고 올리기도 하면 시詩글에 표현이 부족하여진다고 만류를 하는 선배도 있었다.

처음부터 시를 쓸 때 사진이나 그림을 넣던 습관이 되어서 글로만 표현하고 글쓰기가 쉽지는 않았다. 사진과 동영상을 가미하여 유튜브에 올려보기 시작한 것이 계기가 되어서 영상시를 만들기 시작하고 있다.

또「시인처럼 살고 싶다」詩집을 편집하면서 QR코드도 만들어 넣어 보기도 하고, URL주소도 넣어 보았다. 되도록이면 현대문물을 많이 접하려고 애쓰고 있다.

The author's words

Everyone says it's a life that everyone has lived hard looking ahead. I don't know when I'm born in this world and when I'll end my life, but I design the future and make considerable effort for it.

There are people who struggle to leave a name three-way honor, there are people who try to earn wealth and lean on their children to leave a legacy, and there are people who only want their own fun hobbies and health.

Among the various types of life, I do not know which category I belong to, but I have lived hard. As I passed 70 years of my life, several poems were written for me. It may seem insignificant to others, but I tried my best to write.

I have been educated in the analog era for more than 70 years, and by the time I have about 60 poems, I can see pictures and videos. Some seniors discouraged me from seeing and uploading pictures taken while writing poems because of the lack of expression in the poems.

When writing poetry from the beginning, it became a habit of putting pictures or pictures, so it was not easy to express and write only in writing. It was an opportunity to upload pictures and videos on YouTube, so I am starting to make video poems.

I also tried to create a QR code and put in a URL address while editing a poem book, "I want to live like a poet." I'm trying to access as much modern culture as possible.

73세에 첫 시집을 낸다는 것이 늦은 감은 있지만 행정학을 전공하고 경영학을 전공한 사람이 시집을 내고 영상시를 만들다 보니 지각생시인이 되었다. (번역시집)

언제 누군가 나에게 대표 시詩가 무엇이냐고 물었을 때 대답을 선뜻 못하고, 지하철 스크린도어에 걸려있는 시는 「아버지의 쌍지팡이」 시비에 새겨진 시는 「목련 꽃 몽우리」 유튜브에 조회 수가 많은 시는 「어머니를 고려장하다니」 와 「장미꽃 피었네」 라고 하면서 말꼬리를 흐린다.

처음 종로복지관에서 나에게 시詩를 가르쳐준 박정이 선생님과 한국문인협회 부이사장 강희근, 이혜선 교수님이 시詩를 지도해 주신 덕분이다. 특히나 한국문예춘추 이양우 이사장님은 시와 수필을 등단시켜서 용기를 주시고, 문예춘추시인대학 김은자 회장님은 수시로 지도해 주시는데 감사를 표합니다.

내 삶에 가까운 일들을 끄집어내어 짧은 글로써 표현하다 보니 부모님과 형제자매들의 이야기가 자주 등장했다. 글을 뒷받침하는 사진도 올리다 보니 나에게 가까운 지인들의 사진이 자주 올려지기도 하였다.

앞으로 우리들의 한글시가 발전하는 방향은 순수한 우리말 시어가 많이 발굴이 되어야 할 것이며 영상 한영자막 시로 발전할 수 있었으면 한다. 영상으로 한영자막 시를 쓰다 보면 한글 세계화에도 보탬이 되지 않을까 생각한다.

Although it may be too late to have her first book of poetry at 73, she became a late poet after a public administration major and business administration major published a book of poetry and made a video poem. (Translation Poetry)

When someone asks me what the representative poem is, I can't answer it quickly, and the poem hanging on the subway screen door is engraved on the poem "Father's Twin Gables," and the poem, which has a lot of views on the "Magnolia Flower Mongri" YouTube, blurs the words, saying, "How can you consider your mother" and "Rose Blossoms?"

It is thanks to Park Jeong-i, who taught me poetry at the Jongno Welfare Center for the first time, Kang Hee-geun, vice president of the Korean Writers Association, and Professor Lee Hye-sun, who taught me poetry. In particular, Chairman Lee Yang-woo of Korean Literature, Culture, Sports and Literature, and Poetry University Chairman Kim Eun-ja thanked him for his frequent guidance.

As I took out things close to my life and expressed them in short texts, stories of my parents and siblings often appeared. As I posted photos supporting the article, I often posted photos of acquaintances close to me.

In the future, our direction for the development of Hangul poetry will have to be discovered a lot of pure Korean poetry, and I hope that the video will be developed into a Korean-English script poem. I think that writing Korean-English subtitles as a video will help globalize Hangul.

차례 A turn

01 어머니를 고려장하다니 give one's mother Goryeojang 12

02 까치들의 손님맞이 Magpies are welcoming guests. 16

03 예당호 출렁다리 Yedangho Suspension Bridge 18

04 어머니의 지우개 Mother's Eraser 20

05 사진들의 아우성 Screaming of pictures 24

06 시월의 장미 "Rose of October" 26

07 첫걸음 첫 비행 First Step, First Flight 28

08 청계천 잉어 가족 Cheonggyecheon Carp Family 30

09 비둘기 청혼가 Pigeon Proposal Song 32

10 장미꽃에 손님이 Rose and Guest 34

11 어머니 말 한마디에 At the mother's words 36

12 국화꽃 싸움 Chrysanthemum flower fight 39

13 참 좋은 친구들 Very good friends 40

14 눈위에 발자국 Footprints on the snow 42

15 일가구 삼주택 One household, three houses 44

16 장미나목 울타리 Rose Tree Fence 46

17 일어나 앞으로 Stand up. Forward 48

18 고드름 형제들 icicle brothers 50

19 빈집에 손님이 Empty house guest 52

20 눈사람 반장선거 Snowman class president election 54

21 매미들 노래자랑 Cicadas singing contest 56

22 어머니 아픈 손가락 Mother's painful finger 58

23 작은 흰나비 Little White Butterfly 60

24 하루살이 자서전 An autobiography of One Day 62

25 어머니 내음 Mother's smell 64

26 보고 싶은 아버지 I Miss You Father 66

27 아버지 오시는 날 The day my father comes 68

28 병풍 길 융단 길 A folding screen road 70

29 여름 합창소리	Summer Chorus	72
30 짝 찾는 매미	A cicada looking for a mate	74
31 나비여행	Butterfly Trip	76
32 청계천 낚시꾼	Cheonggyecheon fisherman	78
33 전신주, 전봇대	A telephone pole	80
34 가는 길	On the way	82
35 보고 합니다	I'm reporting	84
36 별님과 달님	Star and Moon	86
37 별님과 달님 2	Star and Moon Episode 2	88
38 별님과 달님 3화	'Star and the Moon' Episode 3	90
39 비둘기 생존경쟁	Pigeon survival competition	92
40 단풍잎 정년퇴임	Maple Leaf Retirement	94
41 목련 꽃 몽우리	Magnolia flower budding	96
42 해가 물에 빠졌다	The sun sank into the water	98
43 제라늄 사계절	Geranium Four Seasons	100
44 얼음 나라 봄바람	Ice Land Spring Wind	102
45 봄오는소리	The sound of spring coming.	104
46 어디로 가시나요	Where are you going?	106
47 장미 꽃 몽우리들	Rose-flowering dreams	108
48 장미꽃 피었네	The roses are blooming	110
49 장미꽃 잔치	A rose party	112
50 현충일 전날	The day before Memorial Day	114
51 푸른하늘 하얀구름	Blue sky, white clouds	116
52 삶-장미 어른	Life / Rose Adult	118
53 비둘기 놀이터	A pigeon playground	120
54 능소화의 첫사랑	A trumpet creeper First Love	122
55 청계천 왜가리 외롭다	Cheonggyecheon Heron Is Lonely	124
56 참나리 꽃	Chamnari flower	126
57 어머니생신 케이크	Mother's birthday cake	128

58 어머니의 큰소리   Mother's loud voice   130

59 나는 빚쟁이에요   I'm a debtor.   132

60 칼로 물 베기   Cutting water with a knife   134

61 봄 방울 소리   The sound of spring bells   136

62 빈 둥지   Empty Nest   138

63 어머니는 83세   My mother is 83 years old   140

64 어머니는 주시기만   My mother only gave it to me   142

65 현충원의 아버지   Father of the Memorial Hall   144

66 휴대폰 소리   Cellsound phone   146

67 첫 봄   The first spring   148

68 시/詩   A poem (poem)   150

69 느림보   A slow pace   152

어머니를 고려장하다니

https://youtu.be/0G8pwUKNPSY

어머니를 고려장하다니

너희가 어머니를 고려장 시키고
얼마나 편하게 잘 살려고 그래
너도 70이 넘었으니
똑같이 어머니와 함께 고려장을 시킬까
입이 있으면 말 한 번 해보아라

제가 잘하였다는 것은 아닙니다
어머니가 90이 넘었고 치매가
심하여 손자도 못 알아보고
딸도 못 알아볼 때가 있고
치매 등급이 높아서

가정에서 모실 수가 없고
요양원 시설에서 전문 돌보미가
돌보아야 한다는
병원 진단이 나와서
일등급 요양원에 모셔놓고

전화 통화를 하루에도
몇 십 번을 더 합니다
자식들이 돌아가면서
일주일에 하루만은
어머니를 고향집으로

I can't believe I'm Goryeojang my mother

You're going to make your mother the king of Goryeojang
How comfortable are you trying to live well
You're over 70
Should I order Goryeojang with my mother
If you have a mouth, say it

It's not that I did well
My mother is over 90, and she has dementia
It's so bad that I can't even recognize my grandson
Sometimes, my daughter doesn't recognize me
I have a high level of dementia

I can't take him home
At a nursing home, a professional caregiver
You have to take care of it
I was diagnosed at the hospital
Put him in a first-class nursing home

I talk on the phone every day
I do it dozens of times more
The children take turns
Just one day a week
To my mother's hometown

모시기도 합니다
어머니 조금만 더 기다리셔요
이 아들도 어머니가 계신 요양원으로
들어갈 수만 있으면 바로 들어가서
엄니랑 치매 친구하고 놀게요
어머니를 현대판으로 고려장하다니.

* 옛날 전해오는 동화에서는
  나라 법에 따라 고려장을 시켜놓고
  자식들이 음식을 몰래 갔다 드렸다고 한다.

늙고 병든 부모를 산에 버리는 모습을 묘사한 영화 - 고려장〉

I also invite them

Mom, please wait a little longer

This son is going to the nursing home where his mother lives

If I can go in, I'll go in right away

I'm going to play with my mom and my dementia friend

I can't believe I'm wearing my mother in a modern version.

* In a fairy tale from a long time ago

I ordered Goryeojang according to the law of the country

It is said that the children secretly went to the restaurant.

까치들의 손님맞이

https://youtu.be/j3G_ikY9Ago

까치들의 손님맞이

무슨 회의를 하나

단합대회 인가

비상사태가 아니야

까치들이 한 나무에 다 모였다

귀한 손님이 오신 다기에

접빈사로 마중 나와서

합창으로 야단법석을 뜬다

까치꽃이 만발했다.

Magpies are welcoming guests.

What kind of meeting should we have?

Is it a pep rally?

It's not an emergency.

Magpies gathered in one tree.

A precious guest is coming.

I came out to meet him as a receptionist.

They're making a fuss in the chorus.

Magpie flowers are in full bloom.

예당호 출렁다리

https://youtu.be/S31-HWo6A4s

돌아온 황새가 다리 흔들어서
앞에서 흔들흔들 뒤에서 흔들흔들
마음도 출렁이고 가슴도 출렁되고
다리가 흔들흔들 하늘도 흔들흔들
나도 기우뚱 너도 기우뚱 하늘도 기우뚱

물결도 덩달아 출렁이고 감돌아
무거운 일 어려운 일 흘러내려서
흔들어 다리 줄만 남아, 물은 감돌고
내 마음도 네 마음도 울렁울렁
돌아온 황새가 다리 흔들어서.

예당호 출렁다리

Yedangho Suspension Bridge

The stork that came back shook his leg.
Shake it in the front, shake it in the back.
My heart and heart are shaking.
The bridge will shake, the sky will shake, too.
Me too. You tilt. Sky tilt.

The waves are swaying along with it.
Heavy things and difficult things flow down.
Shake it. Only the rope is left. The water circulates.
My heart, your heart, and my heart growl
The stork that came back shook its leg.

어머니의 지우개

https://youtu.be/63iw45louuA

어머니의 지우개

구십 평생에 지우고 싶은 것이
얼마나 많았을까
둘째 아이를 네 살 때 홍역으로
잃은 것을 팔순이 넘었을 때에도
40이 넘은 막내아들은
삼 남매를 남겨두고
급사를 하니 말 한번 않고
폭주가 시아버지의 술값에
재산은 온대 간대 없어지고
이팔청춘에 쫓겨나기까지 야밤에
학교 교육을 안 받은
고집쟁이 남편과 뜻이 안 맞아
평생을 다투면서 살아
양반 가문에서 일제강점기에
보통학교 교육까지 받았건만
시집 한번 잘못 와서는
화장품 보퉁이를 머리에 이고
이집 저집 행상을 다녔으니 고생고생
어머니 머릿속 지우개는
지울 것이 많기도 하다
땡 고집 영감님이라도 살아있으면
굳세게 싸워보기라도 할 텐데
억압 주던 영감님도

Mother's Eraser

What I want to erase in my 90s and 90s
There must have been a lot
My second child had measles when he was four
Even when I'm over 80 years old
The youngest son who is over 40 years old
With three siblings left
He didn't say a word
The runaway price of his father-in-law's drink
We're going to lose our wealth
Until I was kicked out by 28 years of youth
uneducated
I don't get along with my stubborn husband
I'm fighting for the rest of course
in the Japanese colonial era of the yangban family
I've been educated at a normal school
If you get married once
with a corner of cosmetics on one's head
I've been to different places, so I've had a hard time
The eraser in my mother's head
There are many things to erase
Wrong. If you're still alive
I'm going to have a hard fight hard
The old man who suppressed me

하늘나라로 갔으니 통째로 지워버려
우리 어머니 세상사 한꺼번에
다 지우고 아들딸 보고 싶은
마음만 남겨두고 있다.

He's gone to heaven, so erase it with a whole body
My mother's life all at once
I want to erase everything and see my son and daughter
leave nothing but one's heart behind.

사진들의 아우성

https://youtu.be/i7nr30QDMzU

사진들이 모여 아우성이다
사진 자서전 쓰기 선택에
들어가야 된다고 야단들이다
선택받은 친구는 엄지 척 세운다

선택 못 받은 몇몇 친구들은
삼삼오오 모여서 눈물바람 콧물 바람
아우성이 아니라 결사항쟁이다
이번 선택에서 누락되면
몇 년을 새우잠 자야 될지 몰라

겹겹이 차곡차곡 누워 잠 자야 된다
그곳도 안되면 가위 잘림 당한다
몇몇은 구제하여 줄 테니까
조금 더 기다리라고 달래본다.

Screaming of pictures

The photos are all gathered together.
When I chose to write an autobiography,
They're scolding me that I have to go in.
The chosen one will raise their thumbs up.

Some of the friends who haven't been chosen,
Gather around, cry, runny nose, and wind.
He's not yelling, he's a troublemaker.
If it's omitted from this selection,
I don't know how many years I need to sleep.

You need to lie down and sleep.
If it doesn't work there, you'll get cut off with scissors.
I'll save some of you.
I try to comfort them to wait a little longer.

시월의 장미

https://youtu.be/cPwvfmiAW3o

아파트 앞 울타리에서
늦 장미꽃이 인사를 한다
봄가뭄에 겨우겨우 꽃피웠는데
50일 장마에 꽃잎이 떨어졌다

여러 번의 태풍이 지나가고서
헝클어진 새순 가지치기까지 끝났다
새순에서 시월 늦 장미꽃 활짝 피었다
길고 긴 코로나19도 이겨낸 늦 장미꽃
거리두기하는 빨간 늦 장미꽃이
배시시 웃는 자태가

고고한 학(鶴)의 모습 같기도 하고
세상의 온갖 풍상을 다 겪은
칠십 만학 선비 같다
시월달 붉은 장미꽃 향기는
더 멀리멀리.

"Rose of October"

On the fence in front of the apartment.
The late rose is saying hello.
I barely blossomed in the spring drought.
The petals fell during the rainy season on the 50th.

After several typhoons,
The messy pruning is over.
The roses bloomed in late October from the late October.
A late rose that overcame the long COVID-19.
The red late rose that keeps its distance.
The way he smiles...

It looks like a noble crane.
After experiencing all kinds of customs in the world,
You look like a scholar of 700,000 schools.
The red rose scent of October...
Far away. Far away.

첫걸음 첫 비행

https://youtu.be/WTaz1v1QbKc
자지러지는 까치 어미 울음소리에
까치 새끼도 코 훌쩍여 울고 있다

아파트 앞 화단에서 까치 어미가
이리 날아 보이고 저리 날아 보이고
새끼에게 첫걸음 첫 비행을 시켜본다
날갯짓도 못하고 걸음걸이도 어설픈데
잡식동물인 고양이까지 방해꾼으로

까치 어미는 바쁘다, 안달이 난다
고양이 막으랴 카메라 꾼 막으랴
안전한 집까지 데려가야 하는데
까치 새끼는 아직 날지를 못하고
겨우겨우 몇 발자국 떼고 있다

걸음마에 날갯짓 가르치는 어미
먹여주고 보호하고 아파할까 걱정
부모는 우리를 다 이렇게 키웠지요.

First Step, First Flight

When the magpie's mother cries,
A magpie is sniffing and crying.

The magpie's mother in front of the apartment.
It looks like flying here and there.
I'm going to make him fly for the first flight.
I can't flap my wings and I can't walk.
Even a cat, an omnivore, is a distraction.

The magpie's mother is busy. She's impatient.
Covering the cat and the camera.
I need to take him home safely.
The magpie hasn't flown yet.
I'm barely taking a few steps away.

A mother who teaches how to flap her
wings in her baby steps.
Feed, protect, and worry that it will hurt.
Parents raised us all like this.

청계천 잉어 가족

https://youtu.be/gym6q6MRjmk

어미 잉어가 새끼들 데리고 나와
청계천에서 현장 교육을 시킨다
모래밭 자갈밭 헤집어 주면서
먹을 것과 못 먹을 것 골라보라 한다

삼촌과 이모를 만나면 눈 껌벅이고
꼬리 흔들어서 인사시킨다
원앙새 골짝 왜가리 동네 물 오리촌은
가지 말아라 멀리 나가면 안 된다
물 숲속으로 숨고 납작 돌 아래 찾아

잉어마을 여기저기 뒤져보고 놀아라
다툼도 시비도 없이 왔다 갔다
끼리끼리 만났다 즐겁게 흩어지는
법 없이 살아가는 청계천 잉어마을.

청계천 잉어가족

Cheonggyecheon Carp Family.

Mother carp, bring the babies out
On-site training at Cheonggyecheon Stream
Pushing through the sand and gravel
They want you to choose what to eat or can't eat

When I meet my uncle and aunt, I blink
Wave your tail to say hi
The water duck village in the village of the mandarin
heron
Don't go. Don't go far
Hide in the woods, find under the flat stone

Look around the carp village and play
I went back and forth without quarreling or arguing
We met, and we were happy to be apart
Cheonggyecheon Carp Village, where people live
without laws.

비둘기 청혼가

https://youtu.be/6QhQOZriB6s

비둘기들이 합동으로 맞선을 본다
청계천 오관수교 다리 위에 모여서
고향과 출신 앞으로 계획을 밝힌다
멋진 포즈 자랑하고 노래 부르고
환심을 싸서 웃음을 끌어낸다

이상형 찾았다고 추켜 세워준다
청계천 냇물 따라가면 청혼의 벽이다
종로중구 만남의 다리 위에서 찾아
소프라노 비둘기 " 나를 따라와 봐요"
바리톤 비둘기 "내 사랑받아주오"

청혼의 벽에 바리톤 소프라노 이중합창
나와 결혼해 줘요 언제나 그대 곁에서
먼저 양보하고 큰소리로 사랑만 줄게요
소리소리 높여 청혼가를 부른다.

Pigeon Proposal Song

The pigeons are going to face off together.
Gathering on the bridge of Cheonggyecheon Ogwansugyo
Bridge,
Tell us your plans for the future from your hometown
and hometown.
Show off your cool poses and sing.
He draws laughter by showing his favor.

I'll raise you up for finding your ideal type.
If you follow the stream of Cheonggyecheon Stream,
it's the wall of proposal.
Find it on the bridge of meeting in Jung-gu, Jongno.
Soprano pigeon. "Follow me".
Baritone pigeon. "Accept my love".

Baritone soprano double chorus on the wall of proposal.
Marry me, always beside you
I'll let you go first and give you my love.
Sing the proposal song loudly.

장미꽃에 손님이

https://youtu.be/HVrjB0zYUzY

손님 끌어 모으려고
윙크하고 손 흔들고 발 동동 굴린다
긴 봄가뭄에 물 한 모금 못 마시고
목말라 꽃피우기 힘들었는데

장미꽃에 손님이

50일 장마에 태풍이 겹겹이 온다 하네
장미꽃 고개 수그리고 눈물 뚝뚝
걱정이 되어서 얼굴이 반쪽이다
코로나19 거리두기에 발이 묶였나
꿀벌도 마스크, 나비도 마스크 했다고

손님 없는 좌석에 주인과 직원들만
푸른 제복에 빨간 얼굴 내밀어서
애써 웃음 지으며 손짓한다.

Rose and Guest

To attract customers.
Wink, wave, and roll your feet.
I couldn't drink water in the long spring drought.
It was hard to bloom because I was thirsty.

I heard there will be a lot of typhoons during the rainy
season on the 50th.
Rose, bow your head and knock your tears.
I'm worried, so my face is half the size.
Are you stuck in the COVID-19 distancing?
Honeybees and butterflies are wearing masks.

Only the owner and staff in the seats where there
are no customers.
With a blue uniform and a red face.
He smiles and beckons.

어머니 말 한 마디에

https://youtu.be/U93-DrGuXlc

"왜 이렇게 좋냐 왜 이렇게 좋냐"
지금보다 기분이 더 좋을 수가 있을까
아들딸들이 학교 표창을 받아왔을 때
처음 내가 구의원이 당선되었을 때에도
어머니의 기분이 이만큼 좋았을 것이다
어머니가 십여 년 동안 치매요양원에서

어머니 말한마디에

말 다 잊어버리고 단지 할 수 있는 말
아들딸 보고 싶다 언제 또 볼 수 있나
그 말밖에는 없었다...   그런데
오늘 휴대폰으로 어머니는 큰소리로
"사람 이렇게 묶어 놓으면 법적으로
걸린다 이것은 반드시 고발해야 돼"

2년 동안 아래위 붙은 우주복 입고
붙잡혀서 있다가 처음 하는 말이라
너무 좋아서 큰소리로 외치고 싶다
"어머니 정신이 잠시나마 돌아왔어요"
어머니 또 그런 대화가 될는지 싶어서
휴대폰 걸어보고 또 계속 걸어 본다.

* 아래위가 붙은 우주복을 입히지 않고
붙들어두지 않았을 때 어머니는 넘어져서
크게 다친 경험이 있다.

At the mother's words,

"Why do you like it so much? Why am I so happy?
How can I feel better than now?
When my sons and daughters received school awards,
When I was first elected,
My mother must have felt this good
She's been in a dementia care center for more than a decade
Forget everything you say and just say it
I miss my son and daughter When can we see each other again?
That's all I could say... by the way
Today, my mother shouted loudly on her cell phone
"If you tie people up like this, legally,
You're going to get caught. You have to report this."
For the past 2 years, I've been wearing spacesuits
It's the first time I'm saying this after being held
I'm so happy that I want to shout out loud
"Mother, I came back to my senses for a bit."
Mom, I was wondering if this conversation would be possible
I try to call my cell phone and keep walking.

* without wearing a space suit with the top and bottom on it
When I didn't hold her, she fell down I've been seriously injured.

국화 꽃 싸움

https://youtu.be/8xyzZxOck_k

가을바람 고자질에 화가 난 국화꽃들
노랑꽃 빨간 꽃이 뒤엉켜 싸운다
바람은 편을 갈랐다 붙였다 엉키게 한다
바람의 방향에 따라 엎치락뒤치락

국화꽃 싸움

큰소리치다 손가락질하고 멱살 잡는 꽃들
노랑꽃 찰춤에 코피 터진 붉은 꽃
자빠져서 푸른 제복이 찢어졌다
겨울이 오면 모두가 자멸해야 할 꽃들
내일을 모르고 색깔이 다르다고

이리저리 붙어 줄 섰다가 흩어진다
바람의 방향이 낮과 밤이 틀리니
국화꽃싸움에 찰날은 코미디 마임이다
북 치고 장구 치고 구경꾼들 늘었다
내일을 모르는 청맹과니 내 모습.

Chrysanthemum flower fight

Chrysanthemum flowers angry at the autumn wind.
Yellow flowers and red flowers are tangled and fighting.
Wind split the sides and stuck together. It's going
to get tangled up.
Up and down depending on the wind direction.

Flowers that point their fingers and grab each other's
collar.
Yellow flower. Red flower with a nosebleed.
The blue uniform ripped off.
Flowers that everyone has to self-destruct in winter.
You don't know tomorrow and the color is different.

We stand in line and then we split up.
The direction of the wind is different between day and
night.
In the chrysanthemum fight, the blade is comedy mime.
The number of spectators has increased.
Blue and blind people who don't know tomorrow. My self.

참 좋은 친구들

https://youtu.be/0wMTHgGdtOA

우이령에서 칠십 넘은 참 좋은 친구들
서울있는 고딩친구 고향 꽃이 만발한다
김밥에 목마르면 막걸리 한잔하면은
학창 시절 추억을 더듬어서 헤아려본다

서로의 이름을 불러도 괜찮은 친구
허물없이 농담하여도 웃을 수 있다
나이 들어서 반말할 수 있어서 좋고
가끔은 음담패설 늘어놓아 웃음 짓고
둘레길 걸으면서 손자녀 자랑하면서

세상사 뒤처진 이야기에 열 올려보기도
말동무 길동무에 산 중턱까지 가보자고
괴로움도 슬픈 일도 풀을 수만 있다면
국밥에 소주 한잔하는 친구가 어떠랴
토요일 날에 만나자던 참 좋은 친구들.

Very good friends

Good friends who are over 70 years old in Uiryeong.
My high school friend in Seoul is in full bloom.
If you drink makgeolli when you're thirsty for kimbap,
It's about the memories of school days.

Friends who can call each other's names.
I can laugh even when I joke around.
It's nice to be able to talk informally when I'm older.
Sometimes, I laugh out loud.
While walking along the Dulle-gil, I bragged about my grandchildren.

It's hard to focus on stories that are lagging behind the world.
Let's go to the middle of the mountain.
If I can solve the pain and sadness,
How about having rice soup with soju?
Very good friends that I wanted to meet on Saturday.

눈 위에 발자국

https://youtu.be/UiWtbqbIMBg

첫눈이 밤새 말도 않고 소복이 왔다
온다는 기별이라도 하고 올 것이지
눈길에 발자국 찍으며 노래 불러야지

눈위에 발자국

아무도 다니지 않은 새 길에 첫발자국
발자국 또 발자국 찍으며 앞으로 간다
헤맬 때도 있고 앞선 발자국 따라가다
왔던 길 뒤돌아보다 앞길 묻기도 하지

첫눈 위에 찍힌 희미한 두 발자국
시간 점점 지날수록 지워져가겠지
발자국 남기려고 흔적을 남기려고
돌에 새기고 책으로 남기기도 하네

햇빛 비치면 지워질 줄 알면서도
하얀 눈 왔을 때 좋은 사람 손잡고
첫 발자국을 찍으려 눈밭으로 나간다.

Footprints on the snow

The first snow came without talking all night.
I'm sure you'll at least feel like you're coming.
I'm going to take a step in the snow and sing.

The first step on the new road that no one has walked around.
He's going forward while taking a step.
Sometimes I wander, follow the footsteps of others.
I look back on the way I came and ask for directions.

Two faint steps on the first snow.
As time goes by, it's going to erase.
I wanted to leave a footprint.
I engrave it on a stone and leave it as a book.

Even though I knew it would erase when the sunlight shines on me,
Holding hands with a good person when it snows white.
I go out to the snow to take my first step.

일가구 삼주택

https://youtu.be/e8VBI7J2qcI

저 이는 백 살이 넘었나
집을 셋 채나 가졌어 부자구나
1가구 3주택이야 겨울엔 보여주고
여름에 숨겨버리는 요술의 집인가
느티나무에 까치집이 셋 채다

세컨드 하우스 서머 하우스
아들 집, 딸 집, 손자 집인가
집은 지어도 지어도 모자라고
집이 한 채도 없는 이가 많은데
참 세상은 고르지가 않다

아이들 둘 데리고 전세방으로 갈려다
집주인에게 쫓겨나기까지 했다
월세방 돌다 전세방 갔을 때 기분
오두막집 처음 구입 때 행복을
집부자인 느티나무는 모를 거야.

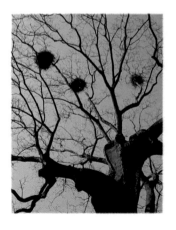

One household, three houses.

Is my tooth over 100 years old?
He has 3 houses. He's rich.
It's one household and three houses. I show it in the winter.
Is it a house of magic that you hide in the summer?
There are three magpies on a zelkova tree.

Second house, summer house.
Son's house, daughter's house, grandson's house.
It's not enough to build a house.
There are a lot of people who don't even have a house.
The world is not even.

I'm going to take two kids to a chartered room.
I was kicked out by the landlord.
How I felt when I went around the rent room and went to
the rent room.
Happiness when I first bought a cabin.
The Zelkova tree, who is rich in housekeeping, will not know.

장미 나목 울타리

https://youtu.be/p9XveWOKW2A

추워 떨고 있던 나목이 눈 이불 덮어
앙상한 가지 생기 넣는 하얀 눈 모자
눈꽃은 아침햇살 올까 봐 걱정되어서
눈물 콧물 훌쩍여 울고 애원하는 눈꽃
뜨는 해와 지는 달 늦출 수가 없구나

장미나목 울타리

해가 지고 또 달이 뜨고 나면
시간 지나 날이 지나 달도 바뀌어서
길고 긴 코로나, 암울한 터널 끝나야
봄 되면 장미 나목마다 새순 돋아나고
따뜻한 봄바람에 장미 줄기, 줄기마다
꽃 몽우리 봉우리 여기저기 달리겠지
장미꽃 나라, 분홍빛 장미꽃 세상에는
벌 나비가 찾아와 윙 윙 하는 꽃 나라
사랑 옹알이는 장미꽃 세상 기다려본다.

Rose Tree Fence

It's cold. My trembling neck covers my eyes
a white hat with a thin branch of life
I was worried about the morning sun
Tears, runny nose, crying and begging snowflakes
I can't delay the rising and falling months

When the sun goes down and the moon rises,
The moon changed over time
Long, long COVID-19, dark tunnel to end
When spring comes, roses come out everywhere
In the warm spring breeze, each stem of a rose

I'm sure it'll run here and there
In the world of roses, pink roses,
A flower country where a bee butterfly comes and wins
Love babbling is waiting for the rose world.

일어나 앞으로

https://youtu.be/yHpB1_FS33E

넘어질 때마다 일어선다
용기 있는 사람은 두려움이 없다
두려움을 이겨내는 사람이 되라

누구나 열정을 다해 노력한다면
위기에 처한 환경도 뛰어넘을 수 있다
성공의 길은 실패하지 않음이 아니라
실패하였을 때 또 일어나는 데 있다
누구든 넘어질 수는 있다

자빠져서 안 일어나면 낙오자가 된다
욕심을 버려라 지금부터 시작이다
우리는 대단한 인간이 아니라
단지 노력하는 한 사람일 뿐이다

앞서기 위해서 대가를 치러 왔으며
앞으로도 많은 이들이 그러할 것이다
최선을 다하면 행운이 따라온다.

Stand up. Forward

He stands up every time he falls down.
Courageous people have no fear.
Be a person who overcomes fear.

If everyone tries their best,
It can surpass the environment in crisis.
It's not that the path to success doesn't fail,
There's a place that happens when you fail.
Anyone can fall.

If you don't wake up, you'll be the loser.
Let go of your greed. It's starting now.
We're not amazing people.
I'm just one person who tries hard.

I came here to pay for being ahead.
Many people will continue to do so.
If you do your best, luck will follow you.

고드름 형제들

https://youtu.be/eXnltLwfkio

하늘을 붙들고 땅이 어디 있느냐
발아래 땅을 두고도 길 물어본다
난간에 손 붙잡고 뿌리를 내릴 건가
살그머니 발아래로 더듬어 보지만

지붕 끝에 뿌리박고 안달복달해 봐도
발 내리는 것이 어설프기는 매한가지
형제들끼리 서로 먼저 내려가겠다고
어깨동무하여 까치발 내려 본다

고드름 형제들

성격도 같고 가는 방향도 같은데
말로는 똑같이 행동하자 약속하고서
찬물 먹고 찬바람 쐬면 배가 부르고
키가 커지고 뚱뚱이 되어간다

겨울이 데리고 온 접 살이 형제들
발가벗고 육체미 자랑하다가도
햇빛 나올까 봄바람 올까
걱정이 태산이다.

icicle brothers

Hold onto the sky and where is the ground?
I ask for directions even if I put the ground under my
feet.
Are you going to take root holding hands on the railing?
I'm slowly fumbling under my feet.

Even if I put roots on the roof and tried to make it dry,
It's hard to put my feet down.
The brothers said they'd go down first.
Put your arms around each other's shoulders and put
your
toes down.

We have the same personality and direction.
Let's act the same way with words. Promise.
If you drink cold water and get cold wind, you'll feel full.
He's getting taller and fat.

The short-lived brothers that I brought with me.
Even though I'm showing off my body,
Will there be sunlight or spring breeze?
I'm worried a lot.

빈집에 손님이

https://youtu.be/SbnKn0IYqh8

문패는 있는데 십 년째 빈집이다
주인은 현충원에 가신지 오래되고
안주인은 강 건너 치매요양원에 살지만
아들딸 앞세우고 집안 점검하는 날에는
키 큰 단감나무 담 넘어보고 인사한다

허리춤에서 대문 열쇠 찾아서 들어서면
영감님 좋아하던 무화과는 주인 따라가고
새로 심은 수박 참외는 손자들이 반긴다
주인이 아끼던 참 나리꽃은 고개 수그리고
포도덩굴도 알맹이 가득 안고 여기 있어요
보라색 가지 많이 컸다고 자랑하네
웃음 잃은 안주인은 아들딸이 웃길 때만
지난날에 꽃밭 가꾸던 모습을 기억하는지

빈집에 손님이

먼 하늘 쳐다보고 주인 영감을 보셨는지
"너의 아버지 어디 가셨노 금방 있었는데"
"돌아가셨잖아요" "나한테 와 말 안 했노"
텅 빈 눈동자에 하늘이 와서 담긴다.

Empty house guest

There's a doorplate, but it's been empty for 10 years.
It's been a long time since the owner went to the cemetery.
My wife lives in a dementia nursing home across the river,
On days when I check my house with my son and daughter in front,
He says hello after crossing the tall sweet persimmon tree wall.

If you find the key to the door in the waist dance,
The fig that you liked followed the owner.
My grandchildren welcome my newly planted watermelon melon.
The flower that the owner cherished was the head down.
The grape vine is full of flesh and is here.
You're bragging that the purple branch grew a lot.
The hostess who lost her laughter only when her son and daughter are funny.
Do you remember how you used to grow flower gardens?

Did you look up at the sky and see the inspiration of the owner?
"Where's your father? He was here soon".
"You passed away". "Come to me. You didn't tell me".
The sky comes into empty eyes and is captured.

눈사람 반장선거

https://youtu.be/44WU62NkqEY

겨울 눈밭에서 큰소리치는 하얀 눈사람
반장이 되겠다고 친구들 불러 모은다
백설 눈사람 뒤이어 자기가 적임자란다
눈사람들 추위보다 선거운동에 열 올려
겨울이 이기려면 하얀 눈송이 합쳐야 해

눈 두 덩이가 뭉쳐질 가능성이 없는데도
서로 흡수하겠다고 주거니 받거니 한다
백설이 가루가 되어서 하얀 이를 돕는다
출마하면 험은 그렇게도 많이 나타나는지
눈도 코도 각각인 눈사람들 제 잘났다고

입은 쳐져 일그러지고 양쪽 팔도 잃었는데
양다리가 다 없고 귀가 둘 다 찢어졌다
장애 있는 눈사람들만 선거에 나왔느냐
성취도 않은 눈사람들이 반장을 한다는데
키 큰 하얀 눈사람을 반장으로 뽑아야지.

눈사람 반장선거

Snowman class president election

A white snowman who shouts loudly in the winter snowfield.
I'm gathering my friends to become the class president.
After the Snowman, he said he's the right person.
Snowmen are more enthusiastic about campaigning than the cold.
In order for winter to win, we need to combine
white snowflakes.

There's no possibility that my eyelids will get cakey.
They're going back and forth to absorb each other's energy.
White snow becomes powder and helps white teeth.
If you run for the election, do you have that many chances?
Snowmen with different eyes and nose are all handsome.

My mouth is sagging, distorted, and I lost both arms.
Both legs are gone and both ears are torn.
Did only the people with disabilities run for election?
I heard that unachieved snowmen become the class president.
I'm going to pick a tall white snowman as the class president.

매미들 노래자랑

https://youtu.be/cQTWQ4NLWJc

칠년 넘게 땅속에서 준비해 나왔다고
맴맴 소리 지르고 또 소리 지르고
전국노래자랑대회에 다들 출전한다
숫 매미 맴돌이 맴석이 맴철이는

일평생 벼루어서 한번 참가하는 기회
방방곡곡 현지에서 예선에 결선까지
심사위원은 맴숙이 맴순이 암 매미들
노래 못 부르면 장가 못 가는 숫 매미
장가가고 싶어서 더위 잊고 악을 쓴다

짝 찾는 노랫소리 애달프다가 슬프다
온 동네에 울려 퍼지게 노래 부르는데
오빠 일등! 하고 맴숙이 날개 흔든다
꼬리까지 흔들고 온몸으로 반긴다.

매미들 노래자랑

Cicadas singing contest

It's been prepared underground for over 7 years.
Shout out loud and shout out loud.
Everyone is participating in the National Singing Contest.
The male cicadas, the male cicadas, the male cicadas.

A chance to postpone and participate for the rest of
your life.
From the preliminaries to finals,
The judges are Maemsook, Maemsoon, and I'm cicadas.
If you can't sing well, you can't get married.
I want to get married, so I forget the heat and use evil.

The sound of finding a partner is sad and sad.
I'm singing all over the neighborhood.
"Oppa, first place!" And wave your wings.
Shake your tail and welcome it with your whole body.

어머니 아픈 손가락

https://youtu.be/d7gvO8JbFaQ

요양원에 계신 치매가 심한 어머니
10년이 넘었어도 자식들이 면회 가면
사진과 자식 얼굴 하나하나 확인한다

어미닭이 품던 계란을 세어보듯이
자식들의 사진을 뚫어지게 쳐다보다
어머니는 보이지 않는 자식을 정확히 골라내서
"둘째는 왜 못 와서 차비가 없었나"
"아니야 둘째는 일이 바빠서 못 왔어요" 해도
"둘째는 생활이 곤란한가 보네 그렇지"

보이지 않는 자식은 계속 물어 본다
어머니에게는 아픈 손가락 !!
어머니에게는 아픈 손가락 !!

Mother's painful finger

Mother with severe dementia in nursing homes.
Even if it's been more than 10 years, if your
children visit you,
Check each picture and face of your child.

Like counting the eggs that a mother chicken had
stare at one's children's pictures
The mother picked out the invisible child exactly
"Why didn't the second one come and there was no bus fare?"
"No, he couldn't come because he was busy"
"The second one must be having a hard time"

The invisible son keeps asking
A painful finger for a mother!!
A painful finger for a mother!!

작은 흰나비

https://youtu.be/oTVMq_I6LBU

나비 한 마리 한꽃에 머무르지 못하고
이 꽃 저 꽃 온 동네를 돌아다닌다
한꽃에 정붙이지 못하고 돌아다닌다

방금 나온 제비나비는 날개가 커서
너플너플 춤추고 잠깐씩 눈인사로
예쁜 꽃들의 시선을 바로 받는다

호랑나비 색깔이 예뻐서 눈에 잘 띈다
인기 나비는 날갯짓하여 훨훨 날아가고
빨간 꽃 노란 꽃 하얀 꽃향기를 뿜으며
꽃잎으로 꽃잎으로 손짓하고 기다린다

작은 흰나비 왔다가는 흔적 남기려니
해는 서산에 기울었는데 갈 곳은 많아
날개가 작은 흰나비 인사할 곳도 많다.

Little White Butterfly

A butterfly can't stay in each flower.
Flowers are all over the neighborhood.
I can't be around a flower.

The swallow butterfly has big wings.
Dancing and greeting each other briefly.
You get the attention of pretty flowers right away.

The tiger butterfly color stands out.
Popular butterflies flap their wings and fly away.
Red flowers, yellow flowers, white flowers.
Gesture with petals and wait.

If a small white butterfly comes and leaves a trace,
The sun is down in Seosan, but there are many
places to go.
There are many places to greet white butterflies
with small wings.

하루살이 자서전

https://youtu.be/kuL0AXdOWLw

하루살이는 하루에 관혼상제 다 치른다
하루를 살다 가면서
자손까지 남기는 하루살이
북 치고 장구 치고 이리저리 날면서
하루 살고 제가 어른이라고
어흠하고 헛기침한다

누가 주인이고 누가 손님인지도 몰라
손님과 주인 회갑 칠순상은 받지 않고
술도 안주도 없이 춤추기에 바쁘다
해가 서산에 기울 때 향연은 절정이다

알과 유충으로 물속에서 일 년 넘게
준비하고 기다렸다고 밤새 잔치한다
잠 깨어난 가로등 아래 모여서 탱고춤
지르박 블루스 육박 춤의 향연이 끝나면
천수 다한 하루살이 무도자의 자서전에
이름 석 자도 못 남긴다는 하루살이.

An autobiography of One Day

A day's worth of ceremonial occasions is a day'
While living a day,
One-day-old man who leaves his descendants.
I was drumming and drumming and flying around.
I live a day and I'm an adult.
I'm coughing in vainly.

We don't know who's the owner and who's the guest.
I didn't receive the 60th birthday award.
I'm busy dancing without alcohol or food.
When the sun tilts in Seosan, the feast is at its peak.

With eggs and larvae, it's been underwater for over a year.
We're going to have a party all night long.
Get together under the street lamp and dance tango.
After the Jirbak Blues Closer Dance feast,
In the autobiography of a heavenly one-day-old dancer,
You can't leave even three names.

어머니 내음

https://youtu.be/5CeOKSD4bK8

어머니 내음 맡고 싶어 1,000리 길 왔는데
코로나 유리벽에 가로막혔어 어찌하나

어머니는 치매로 10년을 요양원에 계셨다
코로나 유리벽 안에서
어머니가 말하는 목소리는 안 들려도
입 모양만 보고 있으면
자식들은 다 알아듣고 대답한다

어머니 내음

요구르트와 간식 싸온 것을 보고
자식들 돈 쓰는 게 아까우신지
도로 가져가라고 한다
지난번에 요구르트 간식을 먹고도
아무도 고맙다는 인사말 아니 하더란다

어머니 내음 맡고 싶어서 1,000리 길을 갔는데
코로나 유리벽에 가로막혔어 어찌할까.

Mother's smell

I want to smell my mom's scent. I came to the 1,000-ri road.
COVID-19 is blocked by a glass wall. What should I do?

My mother has been in a nursing home for 10 years due to dementia.
Inside the glass wall of COVID-19,
Even if you can't hear my mother's voice,
Just looking at the shape of my mouth.
Children understand everything and answer.

I saw him bring yogurt and snacks.
Is it a waste to spend money on your children?
He's telling me to take it back.
When I had yogurt snacks last time,
No one said thank you.

I wanted to smell my mom's scent, so I went 1,000 ri.
I'm blocked by the Corona glass wall. What should I do?

보고 싶은 아버지

https://youtu.be/UF6OpHnl5ns

아버지, 하늘나라에는 전화가 없어요
어머니 보고 싶으면
요양원에 전화하고 찾아가면 되는데
아버지도 하늘 폰 하나 가지세요
아버지 뵈러 가는 날
아침 일찍 목욕하고 아우들 불러 모아
현충원에 가서 참배 드린다

보고 싶은 아버지

아버지 살아생전 사람을 좋아하시더니
돌아가셨어도 친구들이 많으신 아버지
줄줄이 겹겹이 줄 맞추어 우릴 반긴다
아들들 며느리에 딸 사위 왔다고
다음에는 손자들까지 올 거라고
싱글벙글 전우들께 자랑 턱이 만발이다

하나 둘 셋 넷 다섯..... 번호 끝
야간에는 매복하여
단합대회까지 한다는 아버지
호국영령들에 사열 받고
지휘검열관 되어서 하나하나 챙겨 본다
울려 퍼지는 군가 합창 뒤로하고
전우들께 손 흔들어 인사하는 아버지
우리도 하늘 폰 하나 가지세.

I Miss You Father

Father, there's no phone in heaven.
If you miss your mom,
You can call the nursing home and pick it up.
Father, you should have a phone too.

On the day I go to see my dad.
I took a bath early in the morning and called my brothers.
I'll go to the Memorial Hall and pay my respects.

My father liked people all his life.
Father who has a lot of friends even though he died.
They're welcoming us in a row.
My daughter-in-law came to my son-in-law's daughter-in
My grandchildren will come next time.
I'm full of pride to my comrades.

One, two, three, four, five... Number is over.
At night, ambush.
Father who even holds a pep rally.
I was listed by the patriots.
I'll be a commander and censor and watch everything.
Let's leave the chorus behind.
Father waving to his comrades.
Let's have a Skyphone, too.

아버지 오시는 날

https://youtu.be/R5VWZEkC66Y

오늘 향을 피워 아버지를 불러본다
명절에 오시고 오늘도 오시는 아버지
좋아하시던 돼지고기 쌀밥에 과일까지
생시에 드시지 않던 약술도 준비했어요
큰아들 며느리도 이젠 칠순이 지났어요

자식들 어릴 때 손수 팽이를 깎아주시고
통나무 잘라 木 세발자전거 만들어 주던
곰살궂은 아버지, 아들에게는 엄했지만
며느리 넷 아들 넷이 모두 다 모이면
당신께서 먼저 야자타임을 시작하였지요
며느리들 딸들과 즐거워하시던 모습이
향불 앞 영정사진에 아른아른합니다

황천길 불속으로 홀로 들어가실 때에
며느리 넷은 아버지의 관을 붙들고
서로 더 예쁨 받았다고 목놓아 울었지요
사랑을 골고루도 듬뿍듬뿍 주시었나요
사랑을 몰래몰래 통째로 베푸시었나요

오늘은 며느리들이 아버님의 큰 사랑을
첫째 둘째 셋째 막내 자기가 귀여움을
서로가 많이 받았다 자랑하는 날입니다.

The day my father comes.

I'm calling my father with a scent today.
Father who is coming today after the holidays.
Your favorite pork rice and fruits.
I prepared a medicine that you didn't drink before.
My eldest son and daughter-in-law are now.

When they were young, they cut their tops.
He cut the logs and made a tricycle.
He was strict with his father and son.
When all four sons and daughters-in-law get together,
You started Yaja time first.
The daughter-in-law and daughter-in-law had fun.
The portrait in front of the scented fire makes me dizzy.

When you go into the fire alone,
Four daughters-in-law held onto their father's coffin.
We cried because we liked each other more.
Did you give a lot of love?
Did you secretly give out your whole love?

Today, my daughters-in-law gave me a lot of love
The first, second, third, and youngest members are cute.
We received a lot from each other. It's a day to show
off.

병풍 길 융단 길

https://youtu.be/oWlgRvTwoAs

장미꽃 병풍을 쳐 놓은 길
빨간 장미꽃 향수를 뿌려주던 길
님과 함께 오던 길

님과 함께 가는 길
병풍에 꽃잎 따서
축복 융단으로 깔았네
누가 레드 카펫을 깔아 놓았나

어젯밤 이슬이 모자라서
보슬비가 도우고
산들바람도 도와서
합동으로 깔았단다

님과 함께 가는 길
하늘도 바람도, 축복해 준다네.

a folding screen road

a rose-folded road
The road where I used to spray red rose perfume
The way I came with you

On my way with you
I'll pick petals on a folding screen
It's a blessing carpet
Who laid the red carpet

I didn't have enough dew last night
The drizzle helped
I'll help you with the breeze
I put it together

On my way with you
The sky, the wind, bless you.

여름 합창소리

https://youtu.be/YWggoPvnU7c

여름을 뒤흔드는 소프라노 매미소리
아파트 숲속에서 귀를 간지럽힌다
창틀에 붙은 실외기 큰 매미들
위층부터 아래층까지 일렬종대 줄을 서
한 여름 날밤 며칠간을 지휘자도 없이
바리톤으로 합창을 불러 대더니
갑자기 내린 소낙비 소리에
바리톤 큰 매미소리 금방 멈춰있네

들판의 개구리 소리가 듣고 싶고 그립다
귀를 간지럽히는 개구리 소리 듣고 싶다
나, 어릴 때처럼 낮에는 매미소리 듣고
밤에는 개구리 소리 듣고 잠들고 싶다.

여름 합창소리

Summer Chorus

The soprano cicadas that shake the summer.
It tickles my ears in the apartment forest.
Big cicadas on the window frame.
From the upper floor to the lower floor, line up in a row.
On a midsummer night without a conductor,
He sang the chorus in a baritone.
The sudden sound of the rain shower...
The loud sound of cicadas in the baritone stopped quickly.

I want to hear the sound of frogs in the field.
I want to hear the sound of a frog tickling my ears.
Like when I was young, I listened to cicadas during the day.
At night, I want to fall asleep listening to the sound of a frog.

짝 찾는 매미소리

https://youtu.be/XfHYTU2rHrE

폭염이 여기 있어요 여기 있어요
찜염이 덩달아서 덥지요 덥지요
나무숲에서 노래하다가
문 앞에까지 가서 노래한다
낮에 노래하고 밤에는 잠을 자야지
밤낮도 모르나 가려서 좀 울어야
밤새도록 불 켜놓고 잠 못 자게 하니까
보이지도 않게 멀리서 소리만 질러대다

짝찾는 매미소리

나무 껴안고 하소연하다 창문에 대고
견우도 직녀를 만났으니
매미도 짝 만나게 해달라고
짝 만날 때까지

가슴이 아프게 울어야지
가슴이 아프게 울어야지.

- 74 -

The sound of cicadas looking for partners

The heat wave is here. Here it is.
It's hot because of the sauna.
I was singing in the forest.
Go to the door and sing.
I'm going to sing during the day and sleep at night.
Don't you know day and night? You have to cover your
eyes and cry.
Because I can't sleep with the lights on all night.
I just scream from afar so that you can't see me.

I'm complaining while hugging a tree. Put it
on the window.
Gyeonwoo also met Jiknyeo.
I want to meet cicadas too.
Until we meet.

You have to cry heartbreakingly.
You have to cry heartbreakingly.

나비여행

https://youtu.be/t01Z2xDqvm0

빨간 꽃 가보고 노란 꽃도 가본다
정담으로 요기하고 눈인사로 깜박깜박
날갯짓 힘들 땐 잎에서 잠시 잠깐
짝도 친구도 없이 바람이 손짓하면
님을 찾는지 친구를 찾는지 나플나플
날 어두워지면 가지에 걸 터 앉아
비 오는 날이나 달 밝은 밤중에는
나뭇가지 뒤로하고 잎 뒤로 피하면서
갈 때도 올 때도 정해진 곳은 없는데
귀뚜라미 가을 타령에 맞추어서
나비는 바쁜척하고 날기 시작한다.

나비여행

Butterfly Trip

Red flowers and yellow flowers.
With affection, here and blink with an eye greeting.
When you're having a hard time flapping your wings, on
the leaves...
If the wind beckons without a mate or friend,
Whether I'm looking for you or friends, fluttering.
When it gets dark, you sit on the branch.
On a rainy day or a bright moon night,
Put the branches behind you and avoid the leaves.
There's no specific place for me to go or come.
To match the crickets' fall song,
Butterflies pretend to be busy and start flying.

청계천 낚시꾼

https://youtu.be/22MQeFHX53E

긴 목으로 낚시를 한다
길고 긴 시간을 언제나 그 자리에서
고기를 낚는지 세월을 기다리는지
맑은 날 흐린 날 가리지 않고
흐르는 냇물 목 좋은 자리는 잡았지만
낚시 면허증 있는지 없는지
다래끼도 없이 낚시되면 어쩔 것이여
단속도 않고 말리지도 않는 구경꾼들
추운 날 더운 날 언제나 미동도 없이
입질 없는데도 흐르는 물만 보고 있다

청계천낚시꾼

머릿속 가슴속은
덧셈 뺄셈 곱셈까지 바쁘기도 하지
잿빛 왜가리 한 마리
흰빛 왜가리 한 마리.

Cheonggyecheon fisherman

I fish with my long neck.
For a long time, always on the spot.
Whether I catch fish or wait for time.
Sunny days and cloudy days.
The flowing stream. I got a good spot,
Do you have a fishing license or not?
What if I get caught without a sty?
The spectators who don't stop me or control me.
On cold days and hot days, without moving at all times,
I'm just looking at the flowing water even though I don't
have a bite.

In my head, in my heart,
Addition, subtraction, multiplication... I'm busy, too.
One gray heron.
One white heron.

전봇대 전신주

https://youtu.be/apieNKe2ek8

전신주 아가씨가 꽃 훌라후프 하면
큰길에 전봇대 총각도 따라서 돌린다

페츄니아 빨간 꽃 하얀 꽃목걸이하고
봄여름 가을 밤낮을 가리지 않는다
오는 사람 가는 사람에게 기쁨 주고
바람 따라 손짓하여 교통정리까지 해
걸이화분이 하와이 훌라후프 꽃목걸이로
짧은 치마 휘날림에 육감적 눈빛으로
전봇대 단단한 근육질 다리 위 몸통을
허리옷이 번쩍이는 챔피언벨트 되었다

전신주 아가씨가 꽃 훌라후프 하면
큰길에 전봇대 총각도 따라서 돌린다.

a telephone pole

When a utility pole lady hula hoops a flower,
Turn the telephone pole along the main road.

Petunia, red flower, white flower necklace,
Spring, summer, autumn, day and night.
I want to give joy to those who come and go.
Gesture according to the wind and organize the traffic.
The flowerpot is a Hawaiian hula hoop flower necklace.
A short skirt fluttering and with sensual eyes
A telephone pole. A body above a muscular leg.
My waist became the shiny champion belt.

When a utility pole lady hula hoops a flower,
Turn the electric pole bachelor along the main road.

가는 길

https://youtu.be/K1nNXzBNWDY

어디로 어떻게, 어디까지 갈 것인가
길동무에게 물어도, 말없이 그냥 간다
쉬었다 같이 오르자 해도 앞으로 간다

꼭대기 보이냐 물으면 더 가야 된다고
여기가 어디냐 물으면, 다 와 간다고
꼭짓점 어디냐 물으면 손으로 가리킨다

한고비 지났으니, 쉬었다 가자 하면
꼭대기 빙빙 돌아, 어디가 정상인지
여기 짚어보고 또 저기도 짚어보다

지나온 길 뒤돌아보면 아름다웠던 길
꽃 피고 새소리 들으면서, 걸어온 길
칠십 넘었는데도 아직도 진행 중이다.

On the way

Where, how, and how far we'll go.
Even if I ask my friend, he just leaves without saying anything.
Even if I want to go up together after resting, I go forward.

If you ask if you can see the top, you have to go further.
If you ask me where I am, I'm almost there.
If you ask me where the vertex is, I'll point it out with my hand.

After a hard time, let's take a break.
Round and round at the top. Where is the top?
Look here and there.

Looking back on the path, the path that was beautiful
Flowers bloom and listen to the birds. The path I walked on.
It is still in progress even though it is over 70.

보고 합니다

https://youtu.be/D7xd-Dy7ev4

어머니의 막냇손자가 어제 군에 갔어요
중간 손녀딸도 일요일에 시집을 간데요
치매요양원 어머니에 전화로 보고 한다

막냇손자가 해군에 갔어요 보고도 하고
손녀딸 결혼식을 올릴 거라 보고하는데
결혼이란 말도 이름도 성도 잊어버리고
단지 아는 말은, 아들딸이 보고 싶다
한번 볼 수 없나, 같이 살면 안 돼야
알아듣지 못해도 아침마다 전화 올린다
아버지 현충원에 가신 후 후유증으로
어머니는 정신을 놓으시고
치매요양원에 가신지 십 년이 지났다

전화 올리면 못 받는 날이 많을지라도
어머니, 손녀딸이 시집가는 날이에요.

I'm reporting.

My mother's youngest grandson went to the military yesterday.
My middle granddaughter is getting married on Sunday, too.
I'm reporting it to my mother at a dementia care center for dementia.

My youngest grandson went to the Navy. I saw him.
I'm going to have a granddaughter'granddaughter's wedding.
I forgot the name of marriage and last name.
All I know is that I miss my son and daughter.
Can't we see each other? We shouldn't live together.
Even if you don't understand, I call you every morning.
After my father went to the memorial hall,
My mother lost her mind.
It's been 10 years since you went to a dementia care center.

Even if there are many days when I can't answer your call,
Mother and granddaughter are getting married.

별님과 달님

https://youtu.be/LFv30CHhdCU

별님은 윗마을에서 살았고
달님은 아랫마을에서 살았는데
첫눈에 썸 탔어요
두둥실 같이 떠올라
하늘에서 데이트를 했더래요
얼레리 들레리 얼레리 들러리
달님은 부끄러워서 숨고
별님은 달님이 자기 거라고
동네방네 소문냈더래요.

Star and Moon

Byul lived in the upper village.
The moon lived in the village below.
I had a fling at first sight.
It's like floating.
They had a date in the sky.
Hey, hey, hey, hey, hey, bridesmaids.
The moon was shy and hid.
The stars and the moon are yours.
He spread the word around the neighborhood.

별님과 달님 2

https://youtu.be/HvWdQRgb-Io

달님은 별님 생각에 가슴이 울렁인다
온종일 뜬눈으로 새웠어요
별님도 달님 보고 싶어 가슴 조이고
해님이 서쪽 바다로 간걸 보고
둘이는 약속이나 한 듯이
하늘로 두둥실 떠올랐지요
하얀 구름 뒤에서 숨바꼭질하다가
은하수 강 건널 땐 단둘이 손잡고
하룻밤 꼬박 새워서 데이트하였다
이제는 같이 가야 돼
인제는 같이 살아야 돼
내일모레도 별님 달님은 언제나 같이.

별님과 달님 2

Star and Moon Episode 2

The moon's heart flutters at the thought of the stars.
I stayed up all day.
"Fan ID" wants to see you, too. Tighten your chest.
When I saw the sun go to the west sea,
As if you've only made a promise.
I jumped into the sky.
We were playing hide-and-seek behind the white clouds.
When we cross the Milky Way, hold hands together.
I stayed up all night on a date.
We have to go together now.
We have to live together now.
The day after tomorrow, the stars and the moon will
always be together.

별님과 달님 3화

https://youtu.be/KYtQU8SJ9Qg

신랑은 좋아서 싱글벙글 거리고
신부는 연지 곤지 찍어서 달덩이 된다
별님 달님이 한발 두발 맞추어서
하늘로 두둥실 떠오를 때
하얀 구름 뭉게구름 축하객들은
비끼면서 박수로 환호소리 올려준다
칠색 무지개 펄럭이다
꽃비 되어 흩날리고
오색구름도 자리 내어 주어서
은하수 아치형 다리 건널 때는
까치가 무지개다리를 놓았다
레드 카펫을 지날 때는
소낙비 심술꾸러기 멀리서 웃고 있다.

별님과 달님 3화

'Star and the Moon' Episode 3

The groom is happy and grinning.
The bride becomes a moon with Yeonji Gonji.
The stars and the moon will take one step at a time.
When it floats into the sky.
White clouds, clouds. Congratulatory guests...
Move and raise the volume of cheers with applause.
It's a seven-colored rainbow.
It's like a flower rain and it's flying away.
He gave me a spot for the colorful clouds.
When crossing the Milky Way arch bridge,
A magpie put a rainbow bridge.
When you pass the red carpet,
Sonakbi is smiling from afar.

비둘기 생존경쟁

https://youtu.be/Nxee6Gmwgms

생존경쟁이 치열한 비둘기 세상
비둘기세상 인간세상 다른게 없구나
길 위에 비둘기 타고난 운명인가
허겁지겁 달겨 더는 동료와 친구들
먹이 쫓아다니다 내쫓기 바쁘다
쫓기면서도 놓쳐서는 안되는 순간
먹다 들키면 빼앗기고 슬쩍 피하고

비둘기 생존경쟁

푸덕푸덕 날갯짓에 먹이 흘어져
날개 푸덕이다 찢어지고 발가락까지
제 몫 먹고도 욕심부리는 비둘기
비둘기 친구들의 아귀다툼 끝이 없다
생존경쟁이 치열한 비둘기 세상
비둘기세상 인간세상 다른게 없구나.

Pigeon survival competition

The world of pigeons with fierce competition for survival.
There's nothing different in the pigeon world.
A pigeon on the road. Is it a destiny?
Hurry up and hang it up. Colleagues and friends.
Chase after the prey. I'm busy kicking him out.
The moment you can't let go while being chased.
If you get caught eating, you'll be taken away and you'll
sneak away.

Flapping wings, food is scattered.
Flapping wings. Ripped and even my toes.
A pigeon that's greedy even after eating my portion.
Pigeon friends' fight for monkfish is endless.
The world of pigeons with fierce competition for survival.
There's nothing different in the pigeon world.

단풍잎 정년퇴임

https://youtu.be/Me2NddJzHOA

단풍잎 정년퇴임

푸른 제복만 입고 굳세게 일했다
가족을 위하여 하루도 쉬지 않고
한여름 뙤약볕 받으면서 일하고
비바람 맞으면서 변함없이 일했다
일 년 만에 정년퇴임 개근 표창까지
제복이 노랑 옷 빨강 옷으로 바뀌고
정년퇴임 예복 노란색 빨간색이었나
새봄에 가족이 일할 자리 남겨둔 채
입동 바람 팡파르에 다투어 흩날리고
단풍잎 자서전 쓰는 초겨울 날에
하던 일 다 끝내고 떠나는 나그네길
친구들 많아 좋고 동료들 많아서 좋다
내년 봄 새 식구로 돌아올 자리
남겨두고 떠나는 기쁨 마음 설렌다.

Maple Leaf Retirement

I only wore a blue uniform and worked hard.
For your family, without a day off,
I work under the scorching sun in the summer.
I worked hard in the rain and wind.
Including the retirement certificate after a year,
My uniform changed to yellow and red.
Was my retirement uniform yellow and red?
Leaving a place for family to work in the new spring,
Fighting over the fanfare of the winter breeze and scattering it
On an early winter day when I write an autobiography of maple leaves,
I'm on my way home after finishing what I've been doing.
It's nice to have a lot of friends and colleagues.
A place to come back as a new family next spring.
I'm excited about the joy of leaving behind.

목련 꽃 몽우리

봄 몽우리 나왔어
푸른 하늘 간 지려본다
봄이 여기 오고 있다고
소나무 사철나무에 알리고
감나무 느티나무에도
하얀 꽃부터 피우고
푸른 잎도 내놓을 거라고
봄 몽우리 나왔어
푸른 하늘 간 지려본다.

https://youtu.be/JaU21yfWrDU

목련 꽃 몽우리

목련 꽃 몽우리 2
Magnolia flower budding.

Magnolia flower budding.

We got "Spring Dream".
I'm tickling the blue sky.
Spring is coming here.
Let's inform the pine trees.
The persimmon tree, the zelkova tree,
Let's start with white flowers.
They're going to put out green leaves, too.
We got "Spring Dream".
I'm tickling the blue sky.

해가 물에 빠졌다

https://youtu.be/4a9m-EpfgXw

청계천에 해가 빠졌다 강물에도 빠졌다
허우적허우적 헤매면서 나오질 못 한다

물오리도 피해서 지나가고
나르는 비둘기도 그냥 지나간다
가는 사람도 오는 사람까지도
119신고도 않고 건져낼 생각도 없이
지나가면서 하는 말이
지금은 물속에서 헤매고 있지만

해가 물에 빠졌다

내일 아침이면
앞동산에 찬란한 새해가 떠오를 것이다.

The sun sank into the water

The sun has set in Cheonggyecheon I fell into the river
You can't get out of the way while floundering

I avoided the water duck
Pigeons that carry pass by
Even the people who come and go
You don't have to call 119 and get out of here
What I'm saying while passing by
I'm wandering in the water right now,

If it's tomorrow morning,
There will be a glorious new year in the front garden.

제라늄 사계절

https://youtu.be/Wb9k4Z3yAFI

봄이 왔다고 밖에서 알려 준다
창안을 들여다보고 '입춘이 왔어'
베란다에 나란히 앉아서 안과 밖으로
누가 오는지 가는지 밖을 살핀다

제라늄 사계절

티격태격 사랑싸움 구경만 하는 빨강이
사계절 내내 꽃피우며 향기까지 날려
제라늄 향을 피워 자기 몸을 보호하네
한 가지에 봉오리가 생겨서 꽃이 피고

근무교대로 꽃이 피고 꽃 질 때에는
마른 꽃잎도 빨강으로 색깔 잃지 않네
가지치고 몸
단장하면 새색시가 되어
사계절 꽃피우는
제라늄 향기 만발이다.

Geranium Four Seasons

The outside tells me that spring has come.
I looked into the window and said, "It's spring."
Sitting side by side on the veranda, inside and outside.
I look outside to see who's coming or going.

Bickering. Love fight. Red is just watching.
Blooming all year round and blowing off the scent.
It smells like geranium to protect its body.
There's a bud on one thing, and a flower blooms.

When flowers bloom and bloom alternately,
Even dry petals don't lose their color.
Pruning and body.
When I dress up, I become a new bride.
Blooming in all four seasons.
The geranium scent is in full bloom.

얼음 나라 봄바람

https://youtu.be/−9Ac0cK7kyA

단풍잎 흩날리던 우이령 계곡에
얼음과 겨울나무가 서로 뒤 얽혀서
씨름판이 벌어졌다

얼음은 나무를 휘어잡고 늘어지면서
북풍과 한패가 되어서 엉켜 붙는데
나무는 얼음이 힘 빠지길 기다리다
남풍을 기다린다고 목청껏 외친다

칼날 같은 얼음에 찬바람이 도우건만
남쪽에서 봄바람이 몰려서 온다는
소문만 듣고 주눅 들어서 땅속으로.

Ice Land Spring Wind

In the Uiryeong Valley, where maple leaves were scattered,
Ice and winter trees are intertwined.
There's a wrestling match.

The ice is hanging over the tree.
It's tangled up with the north wind.
The tree waits for the ice to run out.
Shout out loud to wait for the south wind.

Even though the cold wind helps with the ice like a blade,
There's a spring breeze coming from the south.
I was intimidated by the rumors and went into the ground.

* music : Spring Rain

봄 오는 소리

https://youtu.be/602pNvU5l1s

경칩 개구리 사랑 찾는 소리에
봄이 오는가 싶어 마중 나간다
목련이 매화를 붙들고

봄이 어디 오더냐 묻는데
연지 찍고 분 바르기 바쁘단다
목련이도 분칠하기 시작한다
개구리 사랑의 세레나데에

매화도 목련이도 몸단장하면서
경칩 개구리 사랑 찾는 노래가
나도 깨우고 너도 일깨운다.

봄이 오는소리

The sound of spring coming.

The sound of finding love for the frog.
I think spring is coming. I'm going to greet you.
Magnolia holds on to plum blossoms.

They're asking where spring is coming.
They're busy putting powder on after putting
on Yeonji.
Magnolia is starting to paint, too.
Frog love serenade.

Plum blossoms and magnolias are getting ready.
The song to find love for frogs.
Wake me up and wake you up.

어디로 가시나요

https://youtu.be/mBWJcBnvU4g

임이여 어디를 가시나요
나를 두고 떠나시나요
우리를 두고 떠나시면서
임의 발걸음이 떨어져요

천 길 만길 머나먼 길로
불 길 속으로, 진정으로 떠나십니까
무엇이 바빠서 서둘러 떠나시오
눈물이 가로막혀서 같이 갈 수 없는 길

살이 미어지는 속울음 들리지 않나요
정녕 가시려면 정이나 띄고 가시지
나는 어찌 살라고 우리는 어찌 살라고
간다는 인사도 없이 그냥 떠나시나요.

어디로 가시나요

Where are you going?

Where are you going?
Are you leaving me behind?
You're leaving us behind
Your footsteps are falling

a thousand ways, a thousand ways, a long way
Are you really leaving, into the fire?
What are you busy about? Hurry up and leave
I can't go with you because my tears are blocked

Can't you hear the whispers of the flesh?
If you really want to go, you should leave me alone
How am I supposed to live? How are we supposed
to live?
You're leaving without saying you're leaving.

장미 꽃 몽우리들

https://youtu.be/xCEFJy8NN5U

장미꽃나라에 선거가 있다고
서로 대표자가 되겠다고
나라에 충성하겠다고
지역주민을 주인으로 모시겠다고
깃발 앞에서 보고하는 꽃 몽우리들
앞으로 누가 공천을 받을는지
누가 끝까지 완주할 수 있을는지
공천 받겠다고 물 밑 작업도
여론조사에서, 좋은 위치에서
빙긋이 웃는 희망찬 꽃 몽우리들.

장미꽃 몽우리들

Rose-flowering dreams

There's an election in the rose country
We're going to be representatives of each other
I'll be loyal to my country
He's going to take the locals as his master
Monks reporting in front of the flag
Who will win the nomination?
Let's see who can finish the race
He wanted to win the nomination
in a good position in the polls
hopeful mongrels smiling.

장미꽃 피었네

https://youtu.be/BEdsawFuVMY

지역주민의 대표자가 되겠다고
깃발 앞에서 공천장 흔들면서
지역주민을 위하겠다고
나라에 충성하겠다고
바람에 소리소리 질러 날려 보낸다
깃발 흔들고 장미꽃도 흔들건만
오던 사람 가던 사람 잡아두지 못하고

가던 길 멈추지 않고 그냥 지나간다.

장미꽃 피었네

The roses are blooming

I want to be the representative of the
local people
Waving the nomination in front of the flag
I'll do it for the local people
I'll be loyal to my country
Shout out in the wind!
I'll wave the flag and the roses
I can't catch the person who came or went

I don't stop on my way, I just pass by.

장미꽃 잔치

https://youtu.be/YbgNkhliK0c

장미꽃의 즐거운 비명소리
딸들은 서로 먼저 꽃피우겠다고
꽃몽우리, 꽃봉우리 눈웃음으로 간지려
첫째가 태어나고 둘째 셋째가 연이어
줄줄이 끝없이 태어난다
딸들이 연달아 줄줄이 태어나서
가슴이 터지도록 기뻤는데

장미꽃 잔치

이제는 딸들마다 저마다
메이퀸 되겠다고 메이퀸이 되겠다고
이웃사촌 딸들까지 세어볼 수가 없네

벌, 나비, 심사관이 오지를 않네.

장미꽃 잔치
A rose party

A rose party

The delightful screams of roses
The girls said they were going to bloom first
A flower bud, a flower bud, it's ticklish with a smile with
his eyes
After the first one was born, the second
and third one were born one after another
Be born endlessly
Daughters were born one after another
I was so happy that my heart exploded

Now, each of the daughters
To become May Queen. To become May Queen
I can't even count the daughters of
my neighbors
There are so many candidates

Bee, butterfly, examiner is not coming.

현충일 전날

https://youtu.be/yVGRZwJ651A

대전현충원에서 11시에 만나자 하고
형제자매들 다 만나자고
조카들 사위들까지 외손도 다 모이네
와 이렇게 좋노 외숙님도 오시네
아버지 혼자 계시다 어머니와 함께 있으니
외롭지 않으시죠
아버지 어머니는 이웃 군병 전우들에게
자랑하고 으슥해한다
아들딸에 며느리 사위가 다 오고
손자녀 손서까지 왔단다
어머니는 85살 남동생이 찾아왔다고
이웃에 떡을 돌리고 웃음꽃이 만발한다
외숙님은 다음에 또 참여하겠다고
치하와 금일봉 띄워줄 때
손자녀 손서들 행복해하고
50년 만의 목마른 가뭄인데도
마른하늘에선 갑자기 구름이 끼고
단 빗방울 날려준다.

The day before Memorial Day

I wanted to meet you at 11 o'clock at Daejeon Memorial
Park
Let's meet all the brothers and sisters
All my nephews and sons-in-law are here
Wow, it's so nice. My uncle is here, too
He's alone. He's with his mother
You're not lonely

My father and mother told my neighboring army
comrades,
He's bragging and getting cold feet
A son and a daughter, a daughter and a son-in-law
I even brought my grandson's son-in-law
My mother said her 85-year-old brother came to see me
Rice cakes are distributed to the neighborhood and
laughter
is in full bloom

He said he would participate again next time.
When compliment and a gift of money are up,
My nephews and sons-in-law are happy
It's been 50 years since I've had a dry spell
In the dry sky, clouds suddenly appear
Blow away the sweet raindrops.

푸른 하늘 하얀 구름

https://youtu.be/i-haaue9Jxk

하얀 구름 청산에 걸쳐서 졸고 있다가
산새도 조용하고 산들바람도 조용해서
보는 이 없다면서 무엇을 하려나
부끄럽지도 않은지 홀라당 벗고 누웠다.

Blue sky, white clouds

The white clouds are dozing off go
The mountain bird is quiet and the breeze
 is quiet
What would he do if he didn't see anything?
I lied down naked, not to be ashamed.

삶 / 장미어른

https://youtu.be/BO2WdhY7u3U

그냥 살라 하네 그냥 살라 하네

때가 되면 꽃피워서
메이퀸이 되겠다는 생각에
찬비 바람에 인고의 나날도
즐거운 희망의 고통으로
새싹이 나올 때 꿈도 많았지
새잎이 나올 때는 꿈도 컸었지
첫째가 피어나고 둘째 셋째
연달아 만발할 때는
꽃향내 소문 듣고 벌 나비 모여들어
하늘이 낮고 세상이 발아래이더라
북 치고 장구 치는 때도 잠시 잠깐
가뭄에 태풍이 몰려와서
꽃잎 떨어지고 송이채로 부러지고
가지자르기까지 당했으니
지난날의 영화는 어디 가고
제2회전 제3 겨우 명분만으로

환갑 진갑에 칠순까지 지났으니
그냥 살라 하네 그냥 살라 하네
하얀 눈보라 덮고서
겨울잠 들 때까지 겨울잠 들 때까지.

삶-장미어른

Life / Rose Adult

He's just telling me to live
When the time comes, I'll bloom
I wanted to be a May Queen
The days of patience in the wind of cold rain
with joyous pain of hope
I had a lot of dreams when the sprouts came out
I had big dreams when new leaves came out
The first is blooming, and the second is the third
When I'm in full bloom in a row,
Bee butterflies gather after hearing rumors of the scent
of flowers
The sky was low and the world was below my feet
When I play drums and janggu, I'll briefly
There was a typhoon in the drought
The petals fall and the pine tree breaks
He's been cut off
Where are the movies from the past?
Round two, round three, just in case

Since I'm past my 60s and 70s,
He's just telling me to live
Covering the white snowstorm
Until I hibernate until I hibernate.

비둘기 놀이터

https://youtu.be/_TQX47IAslM

나비 따라 잠자리 따라
동무들과 놀이터 간다
청계천 강이다
마스크도 없이 빈손이네
보물 찾기를 하나
구석구석 찾아보고
꽃도 따고 벌레도 잡는다
어릴 때 다 이렇게 놀았지
산이고 강이고 들판으로
시간 가는 줄도 모르고
해 저무는 줄 모르고 놀았지
나비 따라가고 잠자리 따라가다
날 저무는 줄도 모르고 놀았다.

A pigeon playground

Following the butterfly and the dragonfly
I'm going to the playground with my friends
It's the Cheonggyecheon Stream
I empty-handed without a mask
A treasure hunt
I looked everywhere
I pick flowers and catch bugs
We used to play like this when we were young
It's a mountain, a river, a field
I lost track of time
I didn't know the sun was setting
follow a butterfly and a dragonfly
I played without knowing that I would die.

능소화의 첫사랑

https://youtu.be/Jzgq6VhpRcA

능소화 꽃이 활짝 피었다
호랑나비는 능소화를 보고
좋아서 빙글빙글 돌기만 한다
능소화도 생글생글 오라고 손짓하고
아! 뿔사 뒤에 있던 꿀벌이
나비보다 먼저 꽃과 입을 맞춘다
꿀벌도 좋아, 나비는 첫사랑으로
꽃잎 피었을 때 시집은 가야지
호랑나비의 마음,
능소화인들 왜 모를까
첫사랑 호랑나비
영원한 나의 오라버니.

능소화의 첫사랑

A trumpet creeper First Love

A trumpet creeper are in full bloom
The tiger butterfly saw a trumpet creeper
I just spin around because I like it
He beckoned me to come to see him
Oh! The bee behind the hornbeam
Kiss the flower before the butterfly
I like bees, too. Butterflies are my first love
When the petals bloom, you have to get married
The heart of a tiger butterfly,
Why don't people know?
My first love, Tiger Butterfly
My brother forever.

청계천 왜가리 외롭다

https://youtu.be/YSp5-SEOdGA
불러주는 이도 찾는 이도 없네
춤추고 노래하는 곳도 없다
짝도 없고 좋아하는 이도 없는데
누구를 잡고 이야기할 때도 없다
찾는 이도 없고 갈데없어도
누가 오는지 누가 불러주는지
만나고 싶어서 다리 길어지고
보고 싶어서 목이 길어졌다
다리 길게 뽑고 목 길게 뽑아
이렇게 살피고 저렇게 살펴본다

혹시! 우연을 핑계 삼아 찾아오려나.

Cheonggyecheon Heron Is Lonely

There's no one to sing it for me or to look for it
There's no place to dance or sing
I don't have a crush or someone I like
There's no time to talk to someone
Even if there's no one to look for and nowhere to go,
Let's see who's coming. Who's
My legs got longer because I wanted to meet you
My neck got longer because I missed you
Pull out your legs and neck
Look at it like this and look at it like that way

By any chance! Will he come by chance as an excuse?

참나리 꽃

아버지 먼 길 떠나가실 때
참나리 꽃도 따라갔다

참나리 꽃은 아버지가 예뻐하시던 꽃
지금은 아들 참나리 꽃이
우리 고향집을 지킨다

텅 빈 고향집에서
어머니와 우리 육 남매를 기다리다
참나리 꽃 목이 길어졌다.

Chamnari flower

When my father left for a long time
The **Chamnari** blossoms followed him

The chamnari flower is
The flower that my father loved
Now, my son's chamnari flower
Protect my hometown

in one's empty home
wait for our six siblings
The neck of the chamnari
flower has lengthened.

어머니생신 케이크

어머니는 1,000리밖에 있는 군인
아들 생일 면회 왔었지요

어머니 생신날 요양원에서
카톡으로 어머니 생신 축하
사진을 보내왔다 1,000리밖에서
"어머니 92회 생신 축하드립니다"
코로나19로 면회도 안 되고
오도 가도 못 하니
봉사자들이 생신 케이크도
준비해 주셨구나
내년 내후년에는 육 남매
다들 모인 밀양 우리 집에서
아들딸들 앞에서 웃음 주고
손자녀들 손뼉 치고 노래부르고
생신 상 받으시고 케이크 자르세요

"보고 싶다 아들아 맛있는
밥 먹고 손도 한번 잡아보자 "

어머니의 손 편지를 오늘도
가슴에서 꺼내본다.

Mother's birthday cake

My mother is a soldier who's only 1,000 ri.
I came to visit my son on his birthday.

On my mother's birthday, at a nursing home,
Happy birthday to your mom through Kakao Talk.
I sent a picture. Out of 1,000 ri.
"Mom, happy 92nd birthday".
You can't visit me because of COVID-19.
You can't go anywhere.
The cake that the volunteers had on their birthday...
They prepared it for us.
In the next year and the year after that,
Everyone gathered in Miryang at my house.
You made me laugh in front of my sons and daughters.
My grandchildren clapped their hands and sang.
Happy birthday and cut the cake.

"I miss you, son. Delicious".
"Let's grab hands after eating".

My mother's handwritten letter.
Take it out of your chest.

어머니의 큰소리

어머니의 큰소리 훈계 또 듣고 싶어요
지난해까지도 큰소리 호통치셨는데
93살 우리 어머니 희미한 기억력에
목소리 점점 작아지고 힘이 빠진

엄니는 회초리를 한 번도 안 드셨죠
회초리 가져오라면 한 아름 드릴게요
어머니 잘 생각해 보세요
자식들 아버지께 야단맞을 일이 생기면
엄니가 먼저 큰소리 우리를 나무라셨죠
병아리를 보호하는 어미닭처럼
그러면 아버지는 헛기침 두 번에
뒷짐지고 나가신다
어머니의 큰소리 훈계 또 듣고 싶어요.

Mother's loud voice

I want to hear my mom's loud admonition again.
You yelled loudly until last year.
My 93-year-old mother's faint memory.
My voice is getting smaller and less energetic.

My mom never ate a whip
I'll give you an armful if you want me to bring
you a whip
Mother, think carefully.
If your children get scolded by your father,
My mom blamed us for making a loud noise.
Like a mother chicken that protects chicks.
Then, my dad would cough twice.
He's holding his hands behind his back.
I want to hear my mother's loud admonition again.

나는 빚쟁이에요

어머니, 나는 빚쟁이에요
어머니는 베풀기만 하셨지요
받으시려고 생각도 아니 하시고
당신께서도 힘들어하시면서
베풀기만 하셨지요
지금에야 알겠습니다

당신께서는 어려운 살림살이도
모진 시집살이도 한 번도 내색 않고
자식은 교육을 시켜야 된다고
무조건, 무조건이었어요
지금에야 알겠습니다
어머니,
나는 갚을 길 없는 빚쟁이에요.

I'm a debtor.

Mother, I'm a debtor.
My mother only gave it to me.
You didn't even think about getting it.
Even though you're having a hard time,
He just gave it to me.
Okay, I got it's okay

You can't afford to live in a difficult house
He never showed his harsh marriage life
Children should be educatedHigh
It was unconditionally, unconditionally
Okay, I got it's okay
Mother.
I'm a debtor with no way to pay back.

칼로 물 베기

자녀들이 모이면
아버지 어머니는 언제나 반대로
서로 자기편 있다고 굴세게 싸웠다
아들네는 말리다 못해 집 나가고
자매들은 울고불고 안절부절

살아생전에 평생을 쌍극으로 다투더니
어떻게 만나서 부부연을 맺었나요
아버지 현충원에 가신 후에는
미운 감정은 다 잊어버리고
부부 꽃이 만발했다

"너희 아버지는 큰소리 한번 안 했다"
"색시와 화목하게 지내라"
어머니는 소싯적 아껴주던 남편 생각에
부부 꽃을 활짝 피우고
당신의 영감 자랑 끝이 없다.

Cutting water with a knife

When the children get together,
Father and mother are always the opposite
They fought hard because they were on their side
I couldn't stop my son from leaving the house
The sisters cry and getting restless

You've been bipolar all your life
How did you meet and get married?
After you go to my father's Memorial,
Forget all the hateful feelings
The couple's flowers are in full bloom

"Your father never said anything loud"
"Be harmonious with your wife"
She thinks of her husband, who she used to cherish
Married flowers in full bloom
Your inspiration is endless.

봄 방울 소리

긴 밤 지나고 봄 **방울** 소리에
홍매화 백매화 화들짝 일어나
양손 흔들고 웃으면서 반긴다

92살 우리 엄니 긴 잠 지나고
봄 **방울**소리에 깨어나서
백매화 홍매화 자연병풍 앞에서
엄지손가락 치켜 세운다
엄마 엄마 내년 내후년에도
이렇게 꽃구경 같이 와야 해요

긴 밤 지나고 봄 **방울** 소리에
홍매화 백매화 화들짝 일어나
양손 흔들고 웃으면서 반긴다.

The sound of spring bells

After a long night, the sound of spring bells
Red plum blossoms. White plum blossoms. Get up.
Wave both hands and welcome them with joyfully.

92 years old, after a long sleep,
I woke up from the sound of spring bells.
In front of the natural folding screen,
I'm going to raise my thumb.
Mom, mom. In the next year or so,
You have to come see the flowers together.

After a long night, the sound of spring bells
Red plum blossoms. White plum blossoms. Get up.
Wave both hands and welcome them with a smile.

빈 둥지

둥지 둥지 지으면서 고생 고생하였다
육 남매를 고이고이 길렀건만
자녀들이 차례차례로 짝을 만나
도시로 떠난 뒤에 두 분께서는
자식들 오기만을 손꼽아 기다리셨다
고집쟁이 영감님은 86세 고개 앞에서
먼저 간다는 말 한마디 못하고
정든 둥지 놔두고 현충원으로 갔다

모두 잃은 안주인은 요양원으로 가면서
"이제는 영영 못 나오는 건가"
"아니야 엄마 병 나으면 나오실 거야"
육 남매 눈물에 떠밀려서 요양원으로
빈 둥지는 십 년을 넘게
오시지도 못하는 주인을 기다린다.

Empty Nest - Lee Sang-geun

You've been working hard building a cabin.
I raised six brothers and sisters.
Children will meet their partners one by one.
After you left for the city, you two
They've been waiting for their children to come.
Stubborn old man, in front of 86-year-old pass,
I couldn't say that I was going to go first.

Your partner and spirit go to Memorial Park
My mother, who lost everything, went to a nursing home
"Can't I come out forever?"
"No, my mom will come out when she gets better".
I was pushed to a nursing home by the tears of six siblings.
My hometown is over 10 years old.

Only the empty nest remains and waits for the owner.

어머니는 83세

현충일 전날은 아버지 제삿날
어머니 모시고 아우들과 제사를 지냈다
현충일에는 어머니 모시고 아우들과
현충원에 계시는 아버지 찾아 참배하고
아우는 어머니 모시고 요양원으로 갔다
어머니는 요양원으로 가시는 도중에

나의 휴대폰으로 전화를 하셨다
"큰아들은 언제 볼 수 있나?"
어머니 어제 집에 오셔서 아버지 제사 지내고
오늘은 현충원에 계신 아버지 뵙고
지금 엄마는 요양원으로 가시는 중이에요
"그러냐."
어머니는 지금 조금도 기억을 못 하신다
어머니 나이 83세 때 아버지께서 돌아가셨는데
아버지 돌아가신지 7년이 지났지만
요사이도 어머니는 83세다. 지금은 모르겠단다

당신의 손자도 못 알아볼 때가 있다
아버지 돌아가시면서 어머니는 정신을 놓으셨다
어머니는 하루 종일 휴대폰으로
6남매에게 전화하시는 게 일이다
"너희들 보고 싶다"   울면서.

My mother is 83 years old.

The day before Memorial Day, my father's memorial service day.
I attended a memorial service with my mother and my brothers
On Memorial Day, I brought my mother and my brothers.
I went to visit my father at the cemetery.
My brother went to a nursing home with his mother.
My mother was on her way to the nursing home.

He called me on his cell phone.
"When can I see my eldest son?"
My mother came home yesterday and held a memorial service
for my father
Today, I met my father at the cemetery.
My mom is on her way to a nursing home.
"Really?"
My mother can't remember anything right now.
My father passed away when I was 83 years old.
It's been 7 years since my father passed away.
These days, my mother is 83 years old. I don't know right now.

Sometimes I don't recognize your grandson.
When my father passed away, my mother lost her mind.
My mom used her phone all day long.
It's work to call six siblings.

"I miss you guys." Crying.

어머니는 주시기만

어머니 키가 작아지셨다
우리가 어릴 때에는
어머니가 키가 더 컸는데

지금은 우리 자식들이 더 커다
우리가 나누어 가졌기 때문에
그래도 어머니는 계속 나누어 준다
어머니는 더 가져가라고 한다

자꾸자꾸 주시기만 하면
우리는 갚을 길이 없는데
울고 싶고 눈물이 난다
어머니는 어떻게 살아요.

My mother only gave it to me

My mom got shorter.
When we were young,
My mom was taller.

My kids are taller now.
Since we shared it,
But my mother still shares it with me.
My mom wants me to take more.

If you keep giving it to me,
We have no way to pay back.
I want to cry and cry.
How does my mother live?

현충원의 아버지

현충원에 아버지 뵈러 가는 날
아침 일찍 목욕하고 아우들 불러 모아
고향에 계신 어머님과 아우들도
현충원서 10시에 모여 참배 드린다

아버지 살아생전에 사람을 좋아하시더니
돌아가셨어도 친구들이 많으시네요
몇 줄로 겹겹이 줄 맞추어 우리를 반긴다
부인과 아들들 며느리에 딸들까지 왔다고
싱글벙글 전우들에게 자랑하며 으쓱해 한다
번호→하나 둘 셋 넷 다섯..... 번호 끝
근무 중 이상 무
아버지, 군병들에게 사열을 받고
지휘검열관이 되어서 하나하나 챙겨 본다

울려 퍼지는 군가 합창 뒤로하고
아버지와 전우들께 하직 인사 올린다.

Father of the Memorial Hall.

On the day I went to see my father at the Memorial Hall.
I took a bath early in the morning and called my brothers.
My mom and younger brothers in my hometown,
We'll gather at 10 o'clock at the Memorial Hall and worship you.

My father liked people all his life.
You still have a lot of friends.
They are welcoming us in a row.
His wife, sons, daughter-in-law, and daughters came.
He brags and shrugs off to his comrades

Number → 1, 2, 3, 4, 5... The end.
I'm fine on duty.
Father, you're being examined by soldiers.
I become a commander and censor and watch everything.

Behind the echoing military song chorus,
I bow to my father and comrades.

휴대폰 소리

휴대폰아 소리 좀 질러봐
너 벙어리 아니잖아
며칠 전까지만 해도
우리 어머니 고운 목소리 잘 냈다
하루에도 30번씩도 더 50번씩까지
그땐 1,000리 밖에 있는 효자였어
왜 어머니 목소리 한 번도 안내냐
지금은 300번이라도 좋다
연거푸 계속이라도 좋아
구십 넘은 울 엄마 목소리
넘어져 다치시고 나서
내가 거는 전화도 잘 못 받네
엄니 쉰 목소리라도 좋아요
우리 엄니 호통치시는 목소리
듣고 싶어서 휴대폰을 쳐다본다.

Cell phone sound

Cell phone, make some noise

You're not a mute.

A few days ago,

My mom made a beautiful voice.

30 times a day or 50 times more

You were a good son a 1,000 ri away.

Why isn't my mom's voice even once?

300 times is good for now.

I don't care if it's continuous

My mom's voice over ninety

After you fall and get hurt,

You can't even answer my calls

I don't care if you have a hoarse voice

My mom's amazing voice

I look at my cell phone because I want to hear it.

첫 봄

청계천 돌다리에 첫봄이 건너온다

어린 봄은 돌다리 건너온 기쁨에

발 동동 구르고 손 흔들고 춤춘다

첫봄의 새싹은 참 예쁘다

어린 봄이 건너오고 또 건너오네
비둘기들도 양지쪽에서 첫봄을 찾는다

사람들도 양지쪽에서 첫봄을 반긴다

물오리와 왜가리도 청계천에서

그들은 첫봄을 찾아서
청계천을 휘젓고 다닌다.

The first spring

The first spring is coming to the Cheonggyecheon
  stone bridge

Young spring is about the joy of crossing the
  stone bridge

Stomping, waving and dancing

The first spring sprout is so pretty

Young spring is coming and coming
Pigeons also find their first spring in the sun

People also welcome the first spring in the sun

Water ducks and herons are also at Cheonggyecheon

They found the first spring
He is wandering the Cheonggyecheon stream.

시 / 詩

너를 찾아 헤매고 있다
산으로 들로 바다로

언제든 어디든 간다
네가 있을 곳이면

웃는 얼굴로 달려갔다가
맥 빠진 걸음으로 돌아오지만

내일도 모레도 헤맬 것이다
너를 만날 때까지.

A poem (poem)

I'm looking for you
Into the mountains, into the fields, into the sea

I'm always going anywhere
Wherever you are

I ran with a smile on my face
It comes back with a discouraged walk

I'll be lost tomorrow and the day after tomorrow
Until I meet you.

느림보

느릿느릿 걷다 보니
구경할 것 많구나
육순 칠순 지나서도
피는 꽃잎 구경하고
크는 열매 더 많이 보네

무지개다리 건너에서
어서 오라 손짓하여도
느림보는 익히고 갈무리하느라
지각생 될 거란다.

A slow pace

As I was walking slowly
There's a lot to see
Even after the 60th and 70th birthday
I'm going to look at the blood petals
I see more fruits

across the rainbow bridge
If you beckon me to come
I learned how to be slow
You're going to be late.

이상근 프로필

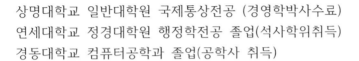

1950년 경남 밀양출생
sam7633111@naver.com

유튜브 : 이상근 TV 채널운영

상명대학교 일반대학원 국제통상전공 (경영학박사수료)
연세대학교 정경대학원 행정학전공 졸업(석사학위취득)
경동대학교 컴퓨터공학과 졸업(공학사 취득)

서울 종로구 구의회 의원
서울청계천복원추진위원회 위원
민주평화통일자문회의 종로구자문위원
성균관대학교 유학대학원 (유림지도자과정수료)

문예춘추 詩 수필 등단
역옹인문학상 수상

삼중당대표

010-5289-3111
02) 763-3111
우편 : 03104
주소 : 서울 종로구 종로5길 7
      (두산a 103동 1405호 창신동)

* '네이버' '다음' 검색창에 '이상근' 검색하시면 참고가 됩니다.